Aloha, I'm 'Alalā the Hawaiian crow, and my green friend is Mo'o the gecko!

Hi! We are members of our school's Geography Club, Hui Hō'ike Honua!

And we are here to help you learn about Hawai'i using maps. It's fun!

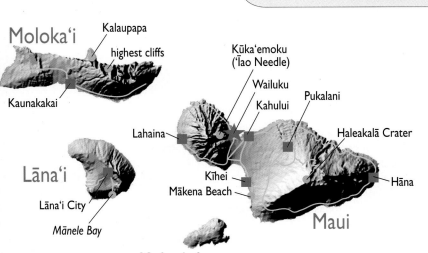

Moloka'i
Kalaupapa
highest cliffs
Kaunakakai

Kūka'emoku ('Īao Needle)
Wailuku
Kahului
Pukalani
Haleakalā Crater
Lahaina
Kīhei
Mākena Beach
Hāna
Maui

Lāna'i
Lāna'i City
Mānele Bay

Kaho'olawe

Map Key

★ **major town or city**
(seat of county government)

■ **town or city**

● **point of interest**

〜 **highway**

Map Scale

25 miles
40 kilometers

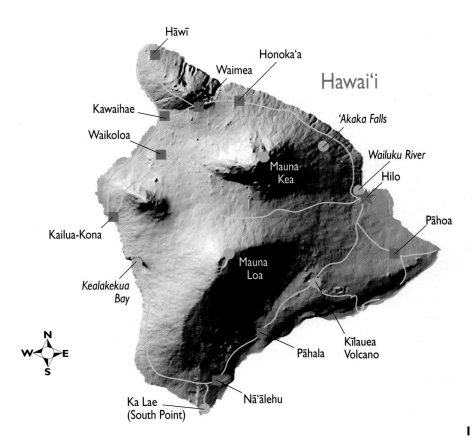

Hāwī
Honoka'a
Waimea
Hawai'i
Kawaihae
'Akaka Falls
Waikoloa
Wailuku River
Mauna Kea
Hilo
Pāhoa
Kailua-Kona
Mauna Loa
Kealakekua Bay
Kīlauea Volcano
Pāhala
Ka Lae (South Point)
Nā'ālehu

N
W E
S

Aloha 'Āina!

1

To the authors' own inspirational geography teachers, respectively

Brigham Arnold
Borden Dent
Sister Mary Bernadette Little

Cartoon characters: Loni Koenig

Design and production: Carol Colbath

Inside cover island chain relief map cartographic and technical assistance: Sandy Margriter, Susan Yugawa and Darin Igawa

Photo credits: Photography by James O. Juvik, except pages 8 (bottom), 9, 14, Air Survey Hawai'i; 11, 38 (bottom), 43 (top), Mark D. Merlin; 15, Jet Propulsion Laboratory; 17 (top), Aloha Airlines; 20, George H. Balazs; 24 (bottom left and top right), *Honolulu Advertiser*; 25 (top two), *Hawai'i Tribune Herald*; 25 (bottom left), J.D. Griggs; 26 (top left), N. Konstantinou; 28 (top), William Mull; 29 (bottom), 30 (top), 31 (bottom right), and 37 (bottom), Jack Jeffery; 30 (center), Sean McKeown; 32 (bottom right), M.A. Tongg; 37 (top) Pacific Whale Foundation; 41 (top center), TESORO Hawai'i; 42 (right), Joseph R. Morgan

Acknowledgments: The authors thank Mary Frances Higuchi and the many public and private school teachers of the Hawai'i Geographic Alliance for their commitment to geographical education in Hawai'i. *Mahalo nui loa* to Haunani Bernardino for reviewing Hawaiian language usage, and to Bacon-Universal Company of Hilo for the use of their steamroller (bottom photo, page 6). We are also grateful for the enthusiasm and cooperation of the many children whose photographs appear in this volume. A special *mahalo* to Bess Press editor Revé Shapard for her assistance in all phases of this project.

Note: Our cartoonist took some artistic license. The real *'alalā* (Hawaiian crow) has a black, rather than a yellow beak.

Library of Congress Cataloging-in-Publication Data

Juvik, James O.
        Student atlas of Hawaii / James O. Juvik,
Thomas R. Paradise, Sonia P. Juvik.
            p. cm.
        Includes illustrations, glossary
        ISBN 1-57306-049-6
            1. Hawaii - Juvenile Literature.
2. Hawaii - Maps. I. Paradise, Thomas R.
II. Juvik, Sonia P.
DU632.2.S78 2000   996.9-dc20

Printed in Hong Kong

STUDENT ATLAS OF

Hawai'i

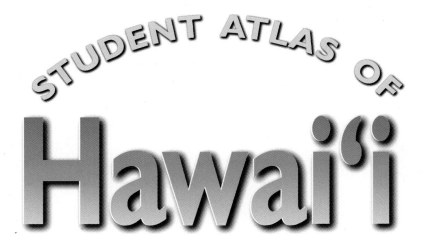

Look where we live in the middle of the Pacific Ocean!

Hui Hō'ike Honua

by James O. Juvik, Thomas R. Paradise, Sonia P. Juvik

Department of Geography & Environmental Studies
University of Hawai'i at Hilo

THE
BESS
PRESS

3565 Harding Avenue • Honolulu, Hawai'i 96816 • (808) 734-7159 Fax (808) 732-3627 • 1-800-910-2377 • www.besspress.com

Kure Atoll

Midway Atoll

Pearl & Hermes Atoll

I like the Northwestern Hawaiian Islands because they are a wildlife refuge for lots of birds!

Hui Hōʻike Honua

Laysan Island

Maro Reef

Northwestern Hawaiian Islands

Gardner Pinnacles

French Frigate Shoals

Table of Contents

When GEOGRAPHERS make a map, they first decide how big an area of the world they want to show on the map. To show where Hawai'i is in the Pacific Ocean they need a map that shows almost half the world! When they focus on a small area like Diamond Head, they can show much more detail on the map.

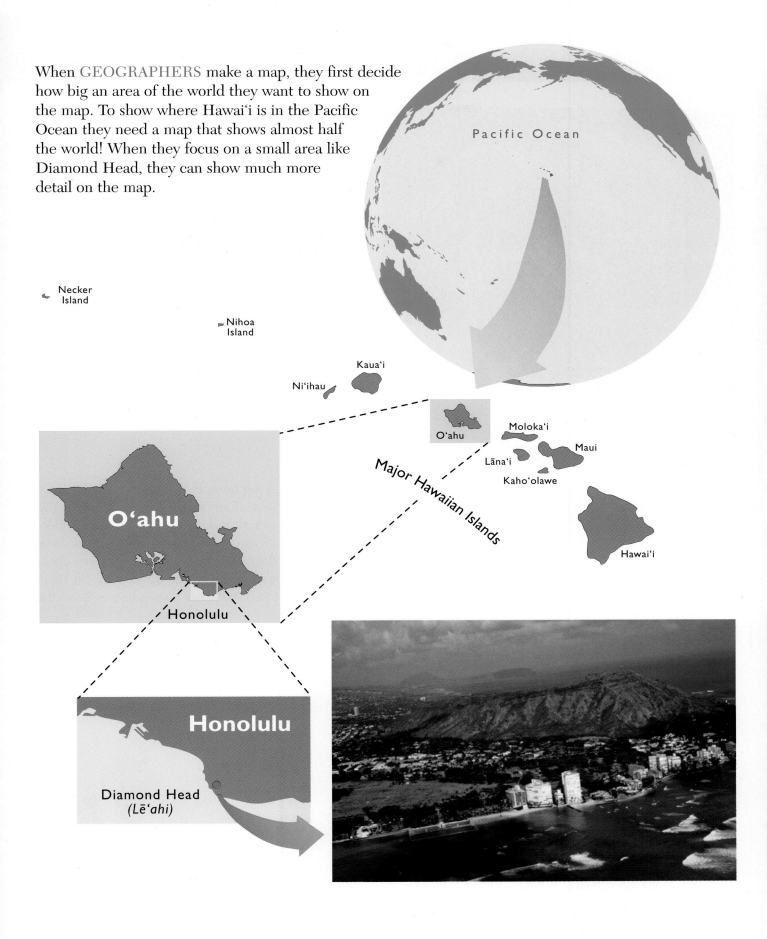

Pacific Ocean

Necker Island

Nihoa Island

Kaua'i

Ni'ihau

O'ahu

Moloka'i

Lāna'i

Maui

Kaho'olawe

Major Hawaiian Islands

Hawai'i

O'ahu

Honolulu

Honolulu

Diamond Head
(Lē'ahi)

Hawai'i

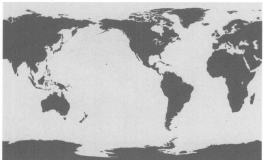

As you know, the Earth is a sphere, somewhat like a ball. Have you tried to flatten the skin of an orange or a tennis ball? You must tear or stretch the skin to make it flat. This is the problem that CARTOGRAPHERS (geographers who make maps) have to deal with in making a flat map of the globe. They make adjustments like those you see in the different world maps on these pages. Look at these maps and compare how each one shows the shape of the land.

Hey! I know how to make a flat map.

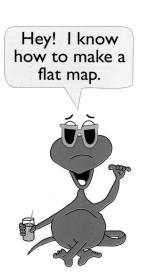

When cartographers show the Earth as a flat map, the different adjustments are called MAP PROJECTIONS. There are many different types. Some projections show the Earth as one single surface, while other projections show slices of the globe.

Let's look at different projections!

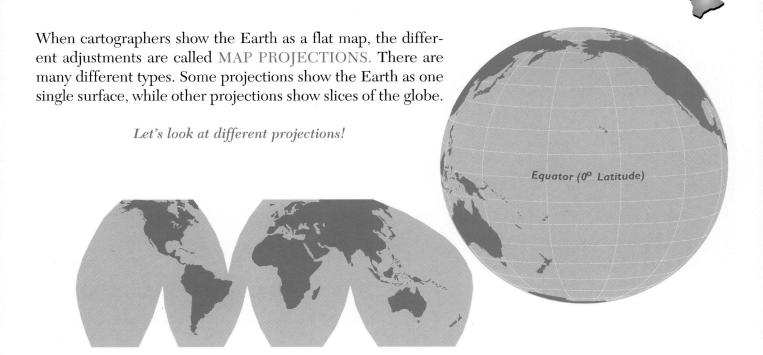

Equator (0° Latitude)

When the globe is flattened to make a map, some areas are distorted, or changed. These changes can be in size or in shape or both. For example, the CONTINENT of South America is nearly six times bigger than Greenland, but on the two map projections below Greenland looks quite different. That's because the edges of the flattened globe must be stretched, and this makes some places appear bigger than they really are. The stretching and distortions show that the globe is still the best way to represent Earth. Even so, people like flat maps because they are much easier to carry and use.

Can you find Greenland and South America and compare the differences in size and shape yourself?

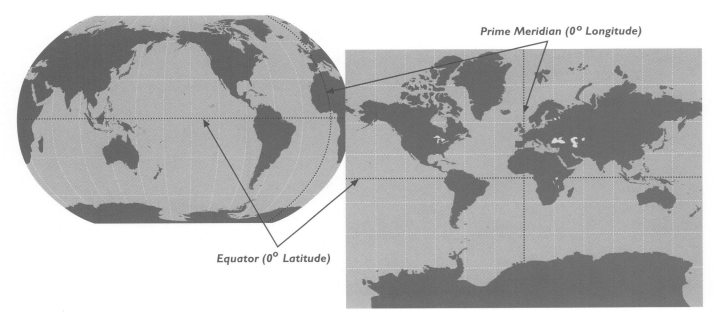

Equator (0° Latitude)

Prime Meridian (0° Longitude)

As we walk along at ground level, we can take photographs of Waikīkī buildings and Diamond Head like the ones above.

But if we photograph the same area from the window of an airplane, we get a different view from above, like the one 'Alalā sees when she is flying high in the sky.

Can you find Diamond Head in this photograph?

A map is like a photograph of an area taken from directly overhead. This is called a vertical view. 'Alalā would call this a "bird's eye view." In a map we use colors, lines, and symbols to represent all the features shown in the photograph. In order to understand what the colors, lines, and symbols on the map mean we need a MAP KEY. The map key makes it easy to "read" the features on the map.

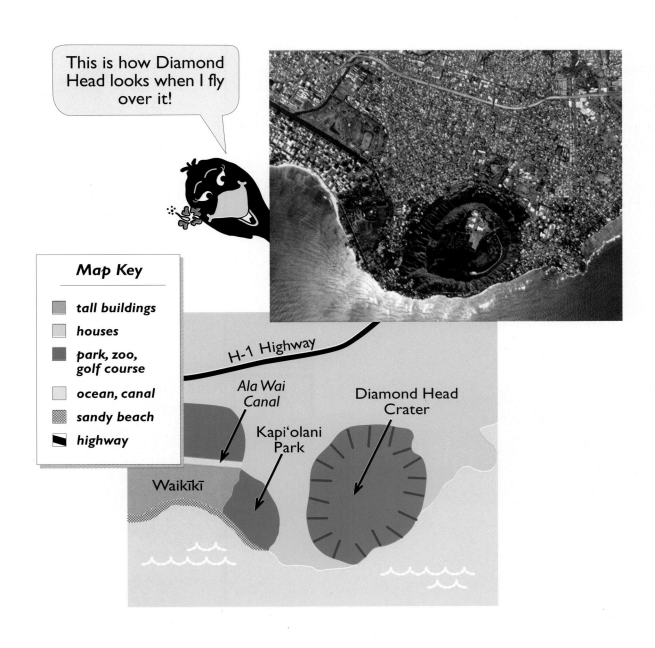

This is how Diamond Head looks when I fly over it!

Map Key

- tall buildings
- houses
- park, zoo, golf course
- ocean, canal
- sandy beach
- highway

H-1 Highway

Ala Wai Canal

Kapiʻolani Park

Diamond Head Crater

Waikīkī

Ni'ihau   Kaua'i

O'ahu

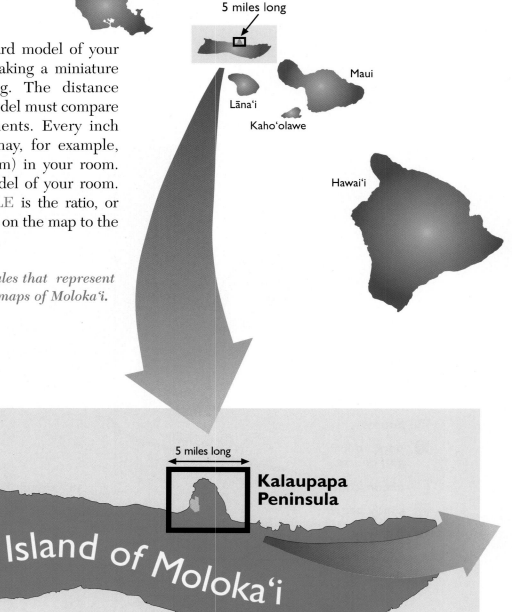

5 miles long

Maui

Lāna'i

Kaho'olawe

Hawai'i

When you make a cardboard model of your room or house, you are making a miniature version of the real thing. The distance between the walls in the model must compare with the actual measurements. Every inch (2.5 cm) in your model may, for example, represent one foot (30.5 cm) in your room. You have made a scale model of your room. On a map, the MAP SCALE is the ratio, or comparision, of the distance on the map to the real distance on the ground.

Look at the different map scales that represent 5 miles (8 km) on the three maps of Moloka'i.

5 miles long

Kalaupapa Peninsula

Island of Moloka'i

The Kalaupapa Peninsula is flat and separated from the rest of Moloka'i by steep cliffs!

5 miles long

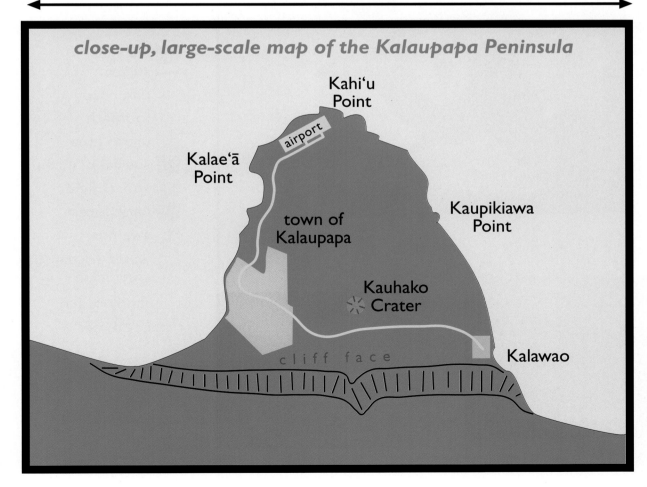

close-up, large-scale map of the Kalaupapa Peninsula

Kahi'u Point

airport

Kalae'ā Point

town of Kalaupapa

Kaupikiawa Point

Kauhako Crater

cliff face

Kalawao

Natural Features

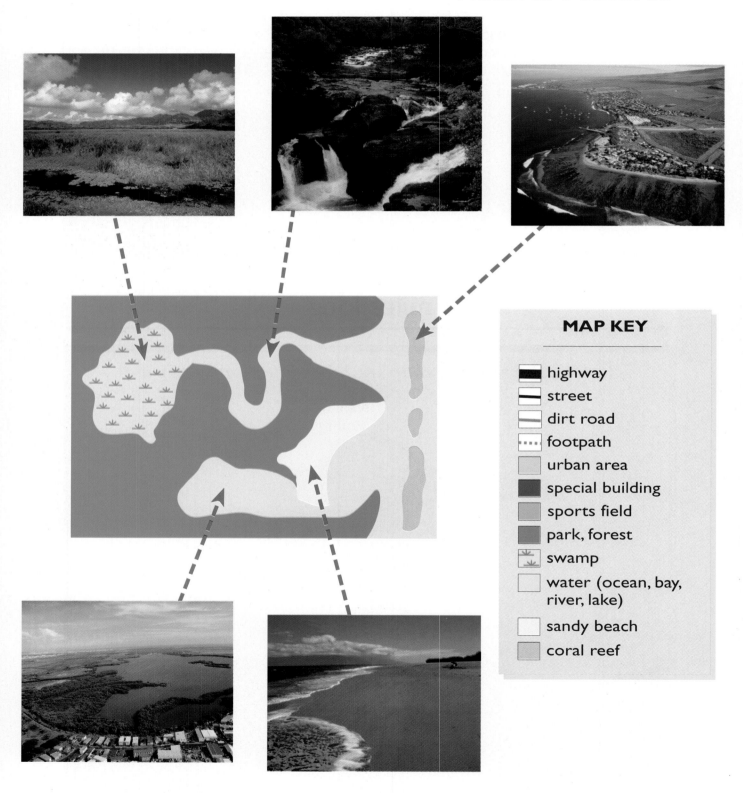

MAP KEY

▬	highway
▭	street
▭	dirt road
⋯	footpath
▭	urban area
▮	special building
▭	sports field
▮	park, forest
※	swamp
▭	water (ocean, bay, river, lake)
▭	sandy beach
▭	coral reef

Cultural Features

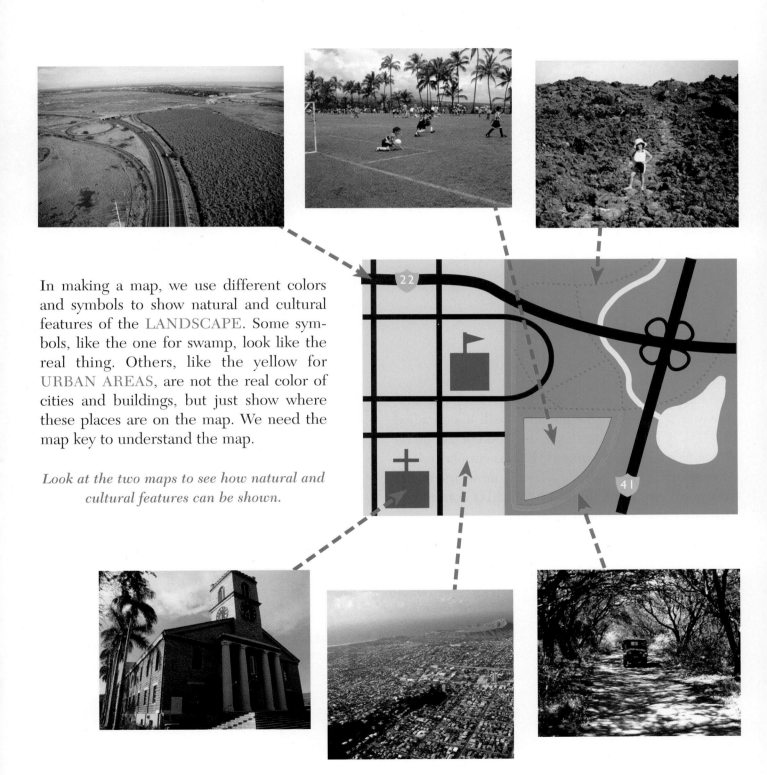

In making a map, we use different colors and symbols to show natural and cultural features of the LANDSCAPE. Some symbols, like the one for swamp, look like the real thing. Others, like the yellow for URBAN AREAS, are not the real color of cities and buildings, but just show where these places are on the map. We need the map key to understand the map.

Look at the two maps to see how natural and cultural features can be shown.

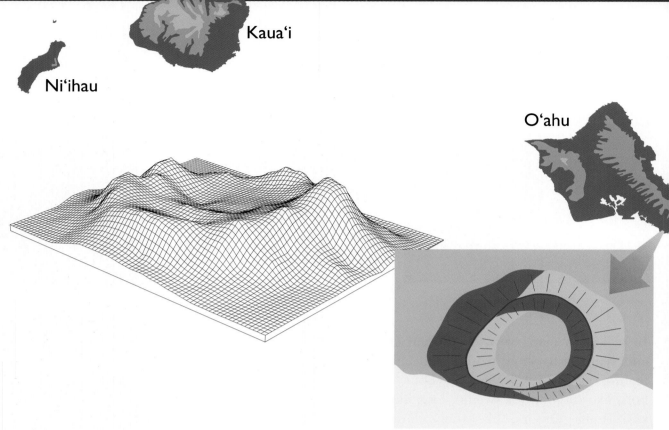

Kaua'i

Ni'ihau

O'ahu

Flat maps can show mountains in different ways. The hand-drawn map of Diamond Head (Lē'ahi), above at right, uses shading and small lines (called HACHURES) to indicate the direction of mountain slopes. We see that Diamond Head is circular, with a depression in the middle. Today most maps are drawn and easily modified with the aid of computers. The map above at left is a computer-generated, three-dimensional view of the same Diamond Head TERRAIN. Below, the highest mountains in Hawai'i are shown in profile, or side view. The elevation, or height, of mountains can also be represented by different colors. Looking at the elevation key on page 15, we can see that the highest mountains on Moloka'i are shaded yellow-green and are 4,000–6,000 feet (1,220–1,830 m) above sea level. Maui and Hawai'i Island have mountains that are above 8,000 feet (2,440 m).

Our Highest Mountains
elevations are in feet (black) and in meters (red)

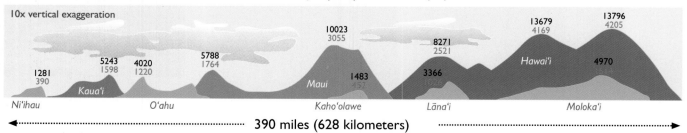

10x vertical exaggeration

| 1281 390 | 5243 1598 | 4020 1220 | 5788 1764 | 10023 3055 | 1483 452 | 8271 2521 | 3366 | 13679 4169 | 13796 4205 | 4970 |

Ni'ihau   Kaua'i   O'ahu   Maui   Kaho'olawe   Lāna'i   Hawai'i   Moloka'i

← 390 miles (628 kilometers) →

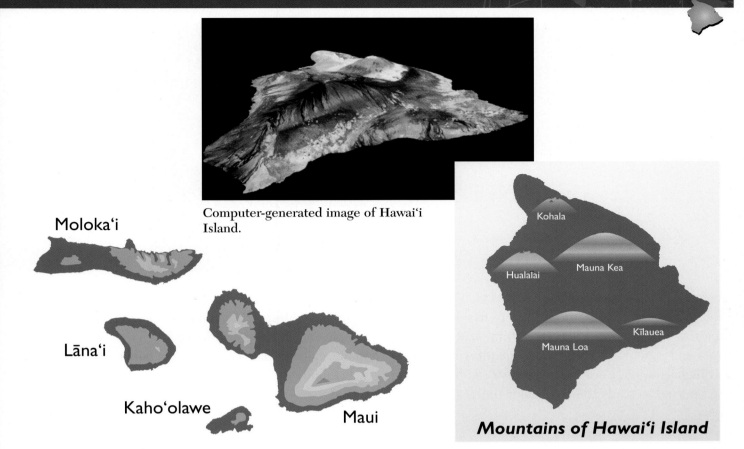

Computer-generated image of Hawai'i Island.

Moloka'i

Lāna'i

Kaho'olawe

Maui

Mountains of Hawai'i Island

Kohala

Hualalai

Mauna Kea

Mauna Loa

Kīlauea

Each color represents a different elevation.

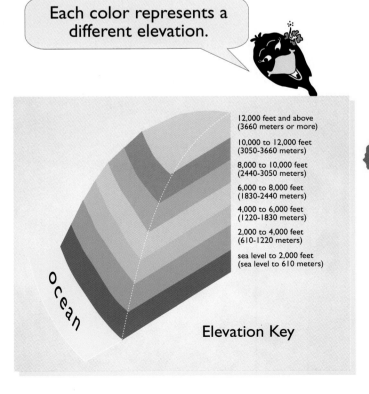

12,000 feet and above
(3660 meters or more)

10,000 to 12,000 feet
(3050-3660 meters)

8,000 to 10,000 feet
(2440-3050 meters)

6,000 to 8,000 feet
(1830-2440 meters)

4,000 to 6,000 feet
(1220-1830 meters)

2,000 to 4,000 feet
(610-1220 meters)

sea level to 2,000 feet
(sea level to 610 meters)

ocean

Elevation Key

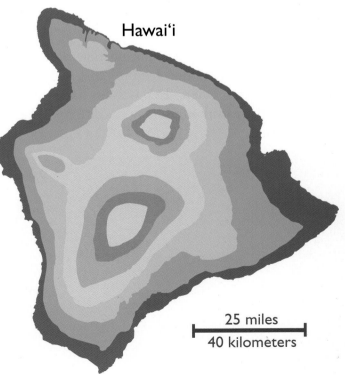

Hawai'i

25 miles
40 kilometers

Districts of Hawai'i Island

Location

Geographers use maps to show SPATIAL DISTRIBUTION. In other words, they use maps to show where things are in the world, both natural features like rivers and mountains and cultural features like cities and highways. On these two pages we see how maps can be used to study the five major themes of geography:

LOCATION tells us where something is found on the Earth's surface. For example, the highway sign in the photograph shows the exact location of the boundary between the South Hilo and Puna districts.

PLACE is a term used to indicate that there are special natural and cultural features that make one area different from others. Hilo is a city, but its size, people, and their work make it a very different place from Honolulu.

MOVEMENT is shown on maps to help us understand how different places are connected. We see how people and things go from one place to another. How many daily passenger flights go between Honolulu and Kahului?

HUMANS AND THE ENVIRONMENT looks at the relationships between the people and the land and how they use and modify it. For example, in the Puna District of Hawai'i Island people clear the forest to build homes and farms.

REGIONS are large areas with features that are alike. For example, the coffee-growing region of Kona, called the "coffee belt," has similar slopes, soils, and climate, and a landscape with many small coffee farms.

Place

Downtown Hilo

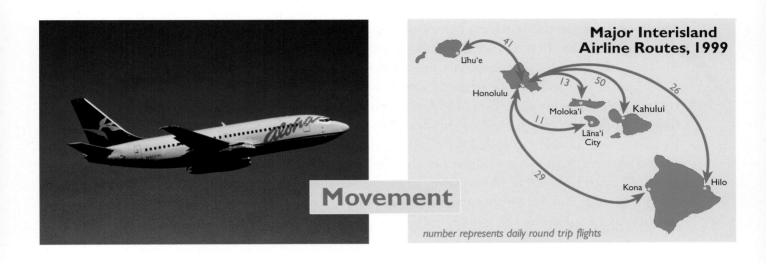

Movement

Major Interisland Airline Routes, 1999

41
Līhu'e
Honolulu
13
50
26
Moloka'i
Kahului
11
Lāna'i City
29
Kona
Hilo

number represents daily round trip flights

agriculture
forest
road
building

Humans and the Environment

Region

Kona coffee-growing region

Island of Hawai'i

Yikes! Look how far away we are from our neighbors around the Pacific!

There are several ways to answer the geographical question *Where are we?* One way is to indicate our position in relation to something else. As you can see in the map below, Hawai'i is west of Mexico and lies in the northern corner of Polynesia. Another way to describe where we are is to show the exact location of Hawai'i on the Earth's surface using LATITUDE and LONGITUDE. This is a grid system using imaginary lines. Latitude is measured in degrees north and south of the EQUATOR, which is at 0 degrees. Lines of equal latitude are called PARALLELS because they run parallel to the equator. Longitude is measured east and west, using lines called MERIDIANS that run from the North Pole to the South Pole. The meridian that passes through Greenwich, England, near London, is called the PRIME MERIDIAN. Its longitude is 0 degrees. The map on page 7 shows the prime meridian. On the map below, we can see that the latitude of Hawai'i is about 20 degrees north of the equator, while the longitude is between 155 to 175 degrees west of the prime meridian. Using this grid system of parallels and meridians, we can determine the exact position of any place on the globe.

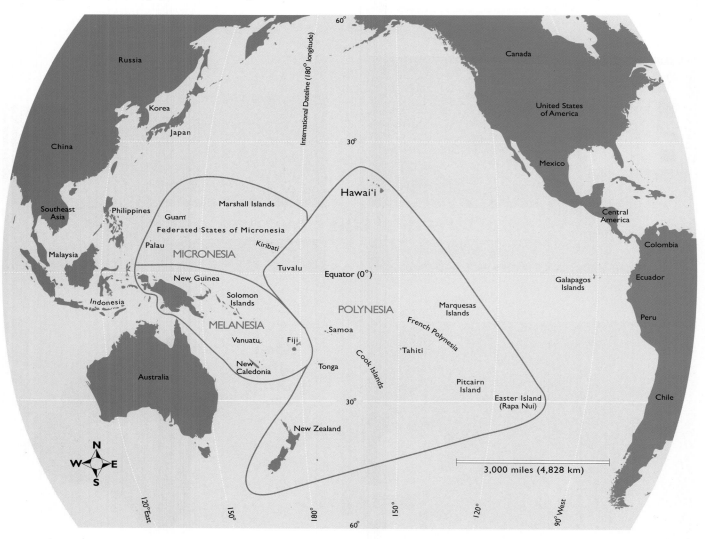

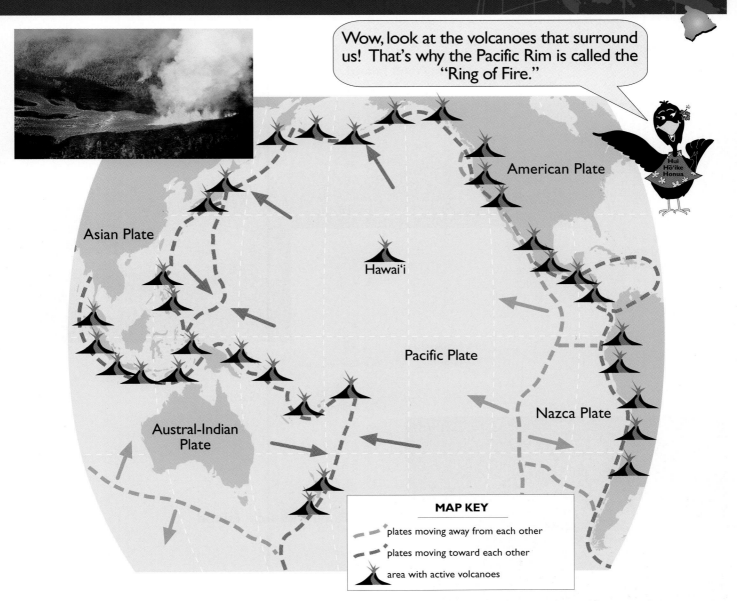

Wow, look at the volcanoes that surround us! That's why the Pacific Rim is called the "Ring of Fire."

American Plate

Asian Plate

Hawai'i

Pacific Plate

Austral-Indian Plate

Nazca Plate

MAP KEY

plates moving away from each other

plates moving toward each other

area with active volcanoes

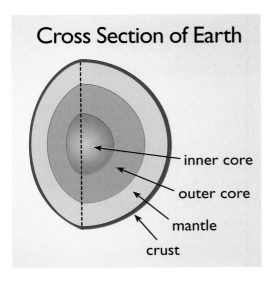

Cross Section of Earth

inner core

outer core

mantle

crust

Where are we? Another way to answer this question is to say that Hawai'i is a group of volcanic islands formed on a giant piece of the Earth's crust called the PACIFIC PLATE. Think of this and other plates as pieces of a very large jigsaw puzzle. These pieces are moving slowly and bump into one another, causing earthquakes and volcanoes. As you can see on the map, most volcanoes occur along the boundaries where the plates crunch together. The volcanoes in Hawai'i are unusual because they are in the middle of a plate. For some reason there is a HOT SPOT in the Earth's mantle under Hawai'i that provides the heat to melt rocks into MAGMA for Hawaiian volcanoes.

The Pacific Plate is moving toward Asia at about 3 inches/year (8 cm/yr).

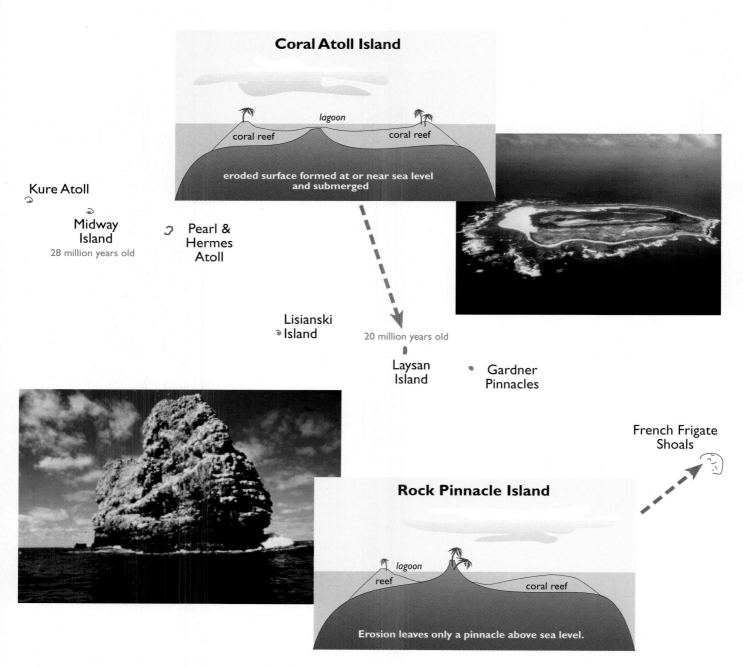

Coral Atoll Island

lagoon

coral reef   coral reef

eroded surface formed at or near sea level and submerged

Kure Atoll

Midway Island
28 million years old

Pearl & Hermes Atoll

Lisianski Island

20 million years old

Laysan Island

Gardner Pinnacles

French Frigate Shoals

Rock Pinnacle Island

lagoon

reef

coral reef

Erosion leaves only a pinnacle above sea level.

The moving Pacific Plate carries the Hawaiian Islands toward the northwest. Islands like Laysan and Midway are far from the hot spot that is now beneath the island of Hawai'i and the nearby underwater volcano Lōʻihi. The older islands no longer have active volcanoes producing lava. On these islands, the forces of rain, wind, and ocean waves working over millions of years cause EROSION.

After a very long time, even large mountains can be worn down into tiny particles and carried away by streams to the ocean. While the volcanoes are being eroded away, living coral reefs begin to grow in the shallow water around the islands. After the volcanoes have completely disappeared, the tops of the reefs remain as small sandy islands called ATOLLS.

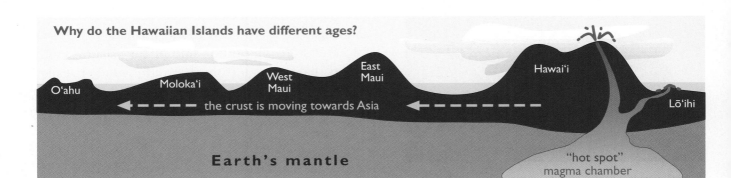

Why do the Hawaiian Islands have different ages?

O'ahu   Moloka'i   West Maui   East Maui   Hawai'i   Lō'ihi

← ----- the crust is moving towards Asia ←

Earth's mantle

"hot spot" magma chamber

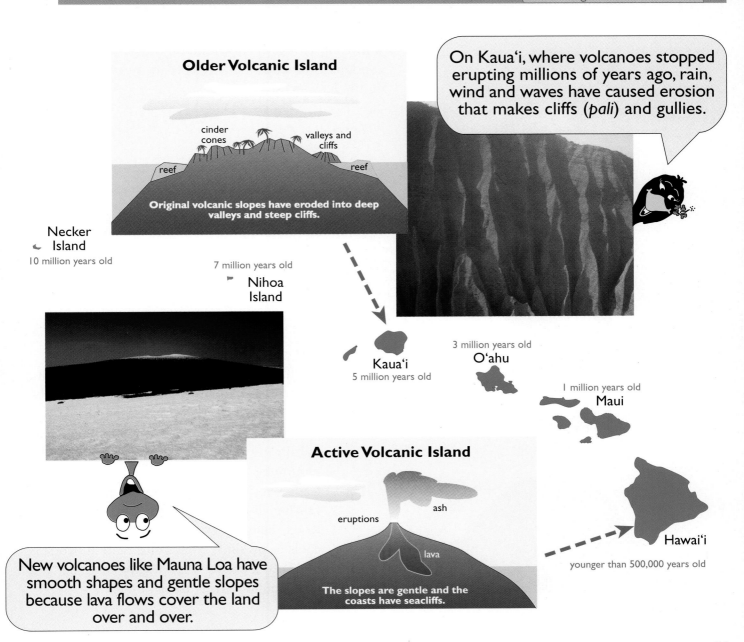

Older Volcanic Island

cinder cones   valleys and cliffs

reef   reef

Original volcanic slopes have eroded into deep valleys and steep cliffs.

On Kaua'i, where volcanoes stopped erupting millions of years ago, rain, wind and waves have caused erosion that makes cliffs (*pali*) and gullies.

Necker Island
10 million years old

7 million years old
Nihoa Island

Kaua'i
5 million years old

3 million years old
O'ahu

1 million years old
Maui

Active Volcanic Island

eruptions   ash

lava

The slopes are gentle and the coasts have seacliffs.

Hawai'i
younger than 500,000 years old

New volcanoes like Mauna Loa have smooth shapes and gentle slopes because lava flows cover the land over and over.

21

Why are some places wet

Tree deformed by strong and constant trade winds at Ka Lae (South Point), Hawai'i Island

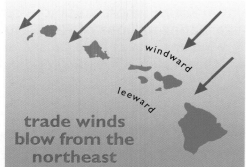

trade winds blow from the northeast

Most of the time in Hawai'i we have winds blowing from the northeast called TRADE WINDS. The north and east areas of each island are called the WIND-WARD side. The other side of the island (south and west), facing away from the trade winds, is called the LEEWARD side. On O'ahu, Kailua and Kāne'ohe are windward, and Honolulu and Wai'anae are leeward.

On the windward side of the islands, as trade winds push air up the mountain slopes, the air cools. This causes CONDENSATION of water vapor into clouds and rainfall. After going over the mountains, the air warms up as it flows downhill on the leeward side and condensation stops. This results in much less rainfall on the leeward side.

Do you live on the windward or leeward side?

The trade winds in Hawai'i blow almost 70% of the time!

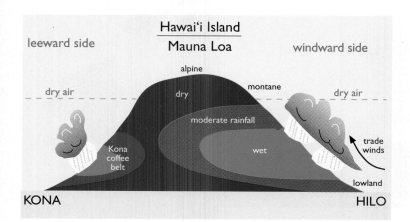

Hawai'i Island
Mauna Loa

On the island of Hawai'i, the mountains are so tall they reach up into dry air above the trade winds. So the tops of Mauna Loa and Mauna Kea have very low rainfall. Snow may fall during the winter months. Because the mountains are very large, they block the trade winds from reaching the Kona region. During the day, the sun heats the slopes in Kona, causing warm air to rise. Rising air cools to produce clouds and rainfall. Kona is the only leeward area in the state that has high rainfall during the summer.

22

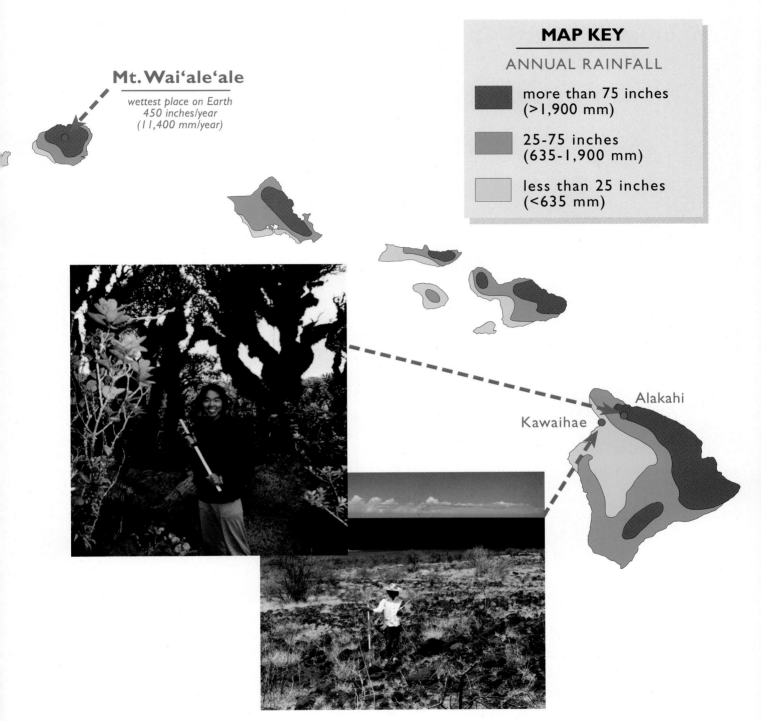

Mt. Wai'ale'ale

*wettest place on Earth
450 inches/year
(11,400 mm/year)*

MAP KEY

ANNUAL RAINFALL

more than 75 inches
(>1,900 mm)

25-75 inches
(635-1,900 mm)

less than 25 inches
(<635 mm)

Alakahi

Kawaihae

At Alakahi, elevation 4,000 feet (1,220 m), on the windward side of the Kohala Mountains, rain and fog occur most of the time, creating a forest where the trees are covered with moss and ferns. This area receives more than 150 inches (3,810 mm) of rain each year. Kawaihae, on the leeward Kohala Coast, is very dry, with less than 10 inches (250 mm) of rain each year. It is like a desert!

Satellite image of Hurricane 'Iniki passing over the Hawaiian Islands

Kaua'i highway after Hurricane 'Iniki on Sunday, September 13, 1992

When an earthquake, TSUNAMI, volcanic eruption, or HURRICANE destroys property or causes loss of life, we call the event a natural disaster. Earthquakes and lava flows related to volcanic activity can be very destructive on the island of Hawai'i, where Kīlauea and Mauna Loa erupt frequently. Earthquakes in Hawai'i and other areas of the Pacific may also produce very large ocean waves called tsunami, which can destroy coastal areas. The atmosphere and ocean may also create other natural disasters like severe storms called hurricanes that produce powerful winds and high waves.

234 people have been killed by tsunami in Hawai'i over the past 100 years!

'Iwa 1982

'Iniki 1992

Dot 1959

Kaua'i

O'ahu

Kahena Street, O'ahu, January 2, 1988, after New Year's Eve flood in Haha'ione Valley

Kahena Street today

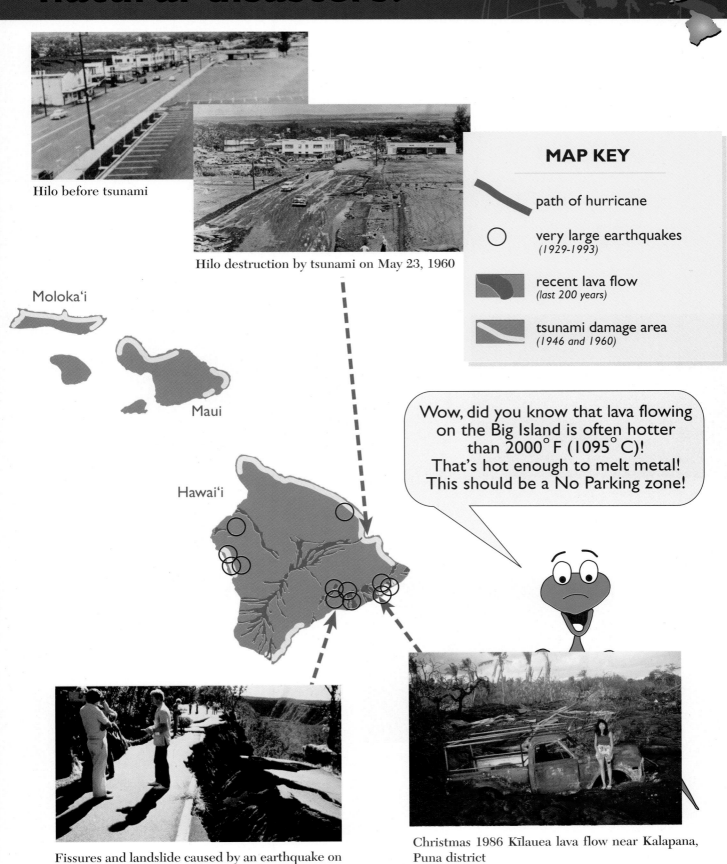

Hilo before tsunami

Hilo destruction by tsunami on May 23, 1960

Moloka'i

Maui

Hawai'i

MAP KEY

path of hurricane

○ very large earthquakes
(1929-1993)

recent lava flow
(last 200 years)

tsunami damage area
(1946 and 1960)

Wow, did you know that lava flowing on the Big Island is often hotter than 2000° F (1095° C)! That's hot enough to melt metal! This should be a No Parking zone!

Fissures and landslide caused by an earthquake on November 16, 1983, at Kīlauea Volcano

Christmas 1986 Kīlauea lava flow near Kalapana, Puna district

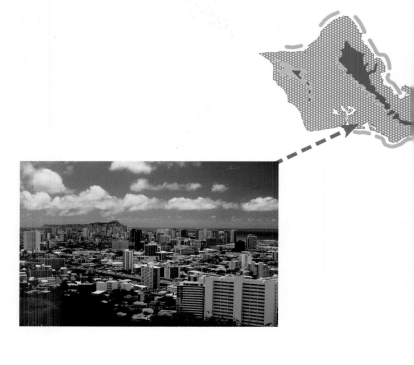

Ecosystems Today

land used by people
(native ecosystems gone)

coral reef

lowland dry forest and grassland

rain forest

upland dry forest and shrub

alpine desert

An ECOSYSTEM is a group of plants and animals living together and using the resources of the physical environment. Scientists have described more than 150 different ecosystems in Hawai'i, which include

- *marine ecosystems such as coral reefs or seagrass beds*
- *aquatic ecosystems such as freshwater streams and lakes*
- *terrestrial (land) ecosystems such as rain forests and grasslands*

Because the climate differs between the wet windward and dry leeward sides of the islands, and between the hot coastal and cool mountain zones, Hawai'i has a great variety of environments where different ecosystems develop.

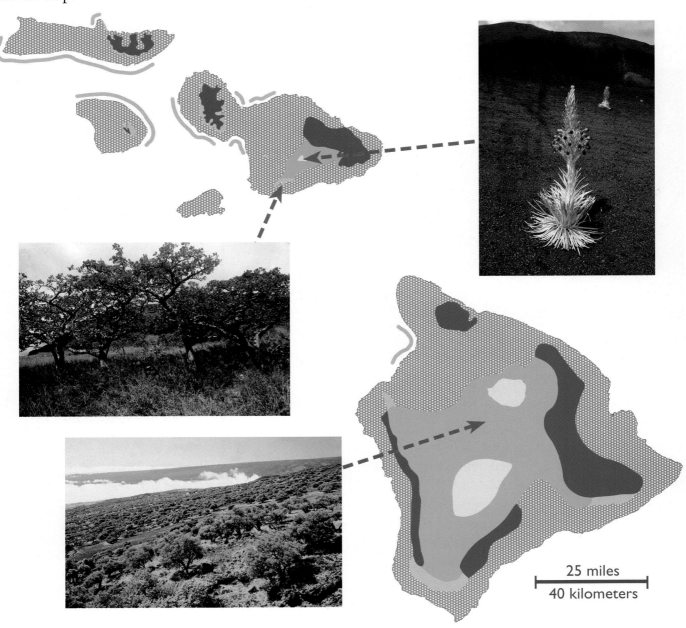

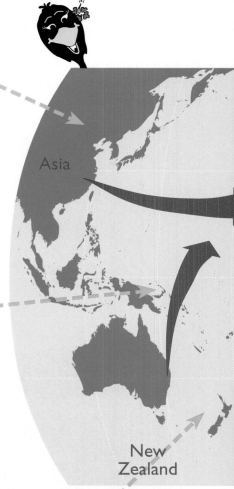

My ancestors flew to Hawai'i long ago before people came. I'm proud to be a native species! But I'm also an endangered species and that makes me sad.

Asia

New Zealand

Tree snails probably arrived in Hawai'i as tiny youngsters stuck to sea birds. This beautiful native snail lives in the Ko'olau Mountains of O'ahu. Tree snails are an endangered species because rats and other alien predators eat them.

The *hala*, or pandanus, tree grows along the coast. Its large seeds float easily and can be carried by ocean currents. This tree is found on many other Pacific Islands.

For millions of years before people arrived in Hawai'i, plants and animals reached these isolated islands by LONG-DISTANCE DISPERSAL. Some animals could swim (turtles or monk seals) or fly (birds, bats, and flying insects) to get here. Plants could get to Hawai'i only if their seeds could float on the ocean, be carried by the wind, or "hitchhike" on birds, stuck to feathers or muddy feet or carried in the bird's stomach.

The *ōhi'a* tree, with its red or yellow flowers (*lehua*) is one of the most common native trees in our rain forest. Its tiny seeds were carried here long ago by the wind from New Zealand and other Pacific Islands.

Plants and animals that came to Hawai'i by long-distance dispersal without the help of people are called NATIVE SPECIES. After they arrived, many of these plants and animals changed through evolution to become new and different species found only in Hawai'i. These are called ENDEMIC SPECIES. When people arrived, they began to change the environment. They cut down forests to plant crops or build villages and, later, big cities. Some of the native plants and animals disappeared (became extinct), while others are now ENDANGERED SPECIES that could disappear if we don't protect them and the ecosystems where they live.

Oops! I don't belong on this page. I'm not a native species!

The 'ōhelo is a native shrub related to the blueberry and cranberry found in North America. The seeds most likely came to Hawai'i in the stomachs of birds.

Many of our native birds were probably blown here by hurricanes or other severe storms. Some birds, like this Hawaiian honeycreeper, 'i'iwi, evolved into new endemic species after reaching Hawai'i.

The mongoose is a native of southern Asia. It was brought to Hawai'i in 1883 to control another alien pest—rats, which were eating the sugarcane crops.

Jackson's chameleons are native to East Africa. They were imported to Hawai'i in 1972 to sell in Honolulu pet shops. Some people turned them loose in the wild.

The first macadamia nut trees were brought to Hawai'i from Australia between 1881 and 1892. Now there are more than 20,000 acres (8,100 hectares) of macadamia orchards in the state.

I'm an alien species. I got here b[y] accident on sailing ships.

Asia

Africa

Australia

Plants and animals brought to Hawai'i by people are called introduced, or ALIEN SPECIES. The first Polynesian settlers brought *kalo* (taro), banana, pig, chicken, and other plants and animals they needed for food. Later, Europeans and Asians brought many other plants and animals from all over the world.

People brought plants and animals to Hawaiʻi not only to raise for food, but sometimes just because they were beautiful (orchids) or made good pets (cats, parrots, goldfish). Some plants and animals arrived here by accident. Rats came as stowaways on sailing ships. Some alien species have become household pests (cockroaches, ants) or may threaten the survival of native species. The mongoose eats the eggs and chicks of the *nēnē*, our native goose.

English explorer George Vancouver brought the first sheep and cattle to Hawaiʻi in 1793. They were allowed to go wild, and they destroyed large areas of native forest.

The guava tree was introduced from South America and now is a pest species that invades native forest areas.

There were no mosquitoes in Hawaiʻi until 1826, when a visiting sailing ship from Mexico emptied water barrels containing mosquito larvae at Lahaina, Maui. Mosquitoes carry diseases that kill native birds.

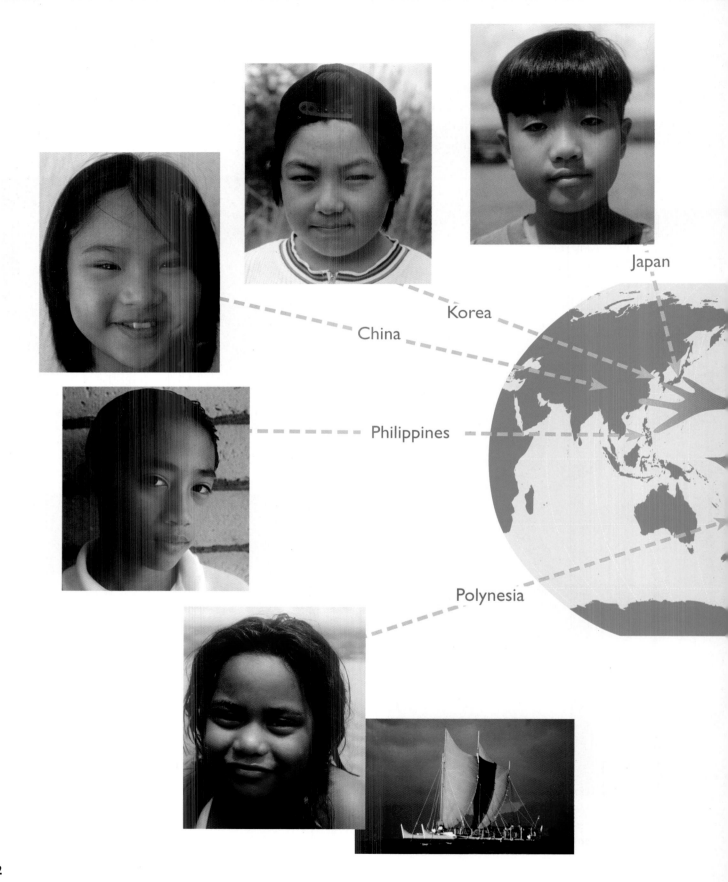

Japan

Korea

China

Philippines

Polynesia

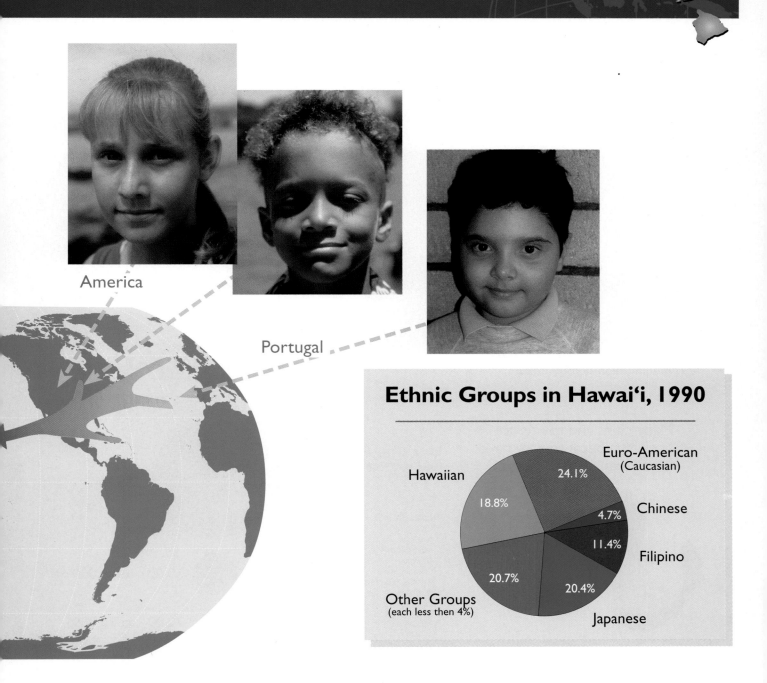

America

Portugal

Ethnic Groups in Hawai'i, 1990

Hawaiian 18.8%

Euro-American (Caucasian) 24.1%

Chinese 4.7%

Filipino 11.4%

Japanese 20.4%

Other Groups (each less then 4%) 20.7%

There are many reasons why people MIGRATE, or leave their places of birth to find new homes. About 1500–1800 years ago, Polynesian explorers sailed from the South Pacific to discover Hawai'i. These first settlers became the Hawaiian people, with their unique language and culture. After Captain Cook arrived in 1778, Hawai'i became known to the rest of the world. Later, in the 19th century, sugarcane and pineapple plantations developed rapidly, and laborers were brought in from many countries like China, Portugal, Japan, the Philippines, Korea, Puerto Rico, and other Pacific Islands. Today, many ETHNIC GROUPS live together in Hawai'i.

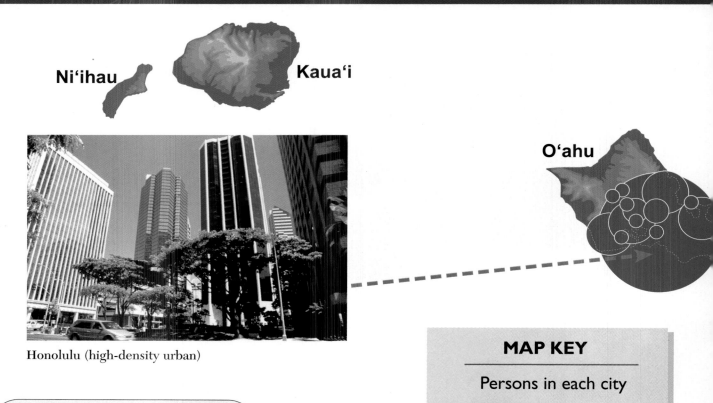

Ni'ihau

Kaua'i

O'ahu

Honolulu (high-density urban)

Many cities and towns are not shown because they have fewer than 10,000 people.

Our Biggest Cities
(More than 10,000 people, 1990)

Honolulu	377,059
Hilo	37,808
Kailua, O'ahu	36,818
Kāne'ohe	35,448
Waipahu	31,435
Pearl City	30,993
Waimalu	29,967
Mililani Town	29,359
Schofield Barracks	19,597
Wahiawā	17,386
Kahului	16,889
'Ewa Beach	14,315
Hālawa	13,408
Waipi'o	11,812
Mōkapu	11,662
Kīhei	11,107
Wailuku	10,688

MAP KEY

Persons in each city

380,000

30,001 to 40,000

20,001 to 30,000

10,000 to 20,000

Almost 90 percent of the people in Hawai'i live in cities. As you can see from the map, most people live on O'ahu. Now 80 percent of the state's 1.2 million residents live there, because most of the jobs are on O'ahu–in offices and banks downtown, in hotels in Waikīkī, in shops and malls, and in the military at Pearl Harbor and in central O'ahu. With its pleasant climate, abundant water supply, and excellent harbor, Honolulu was destined to become the state capital and the leading city in Hawai'i. After 1809, King Kamehameha I moved his court to Honolulu, and the city grew to become the main commercial and governmental center of the kingdom.

Why are the circles on only O'ahu, Maui, and Hawai'i?

Look at how people live close together in the same place! From the size of the circle, you can see how many people live in each city or town. I'm holding a circle that represents 30,001 to 40,000 people.

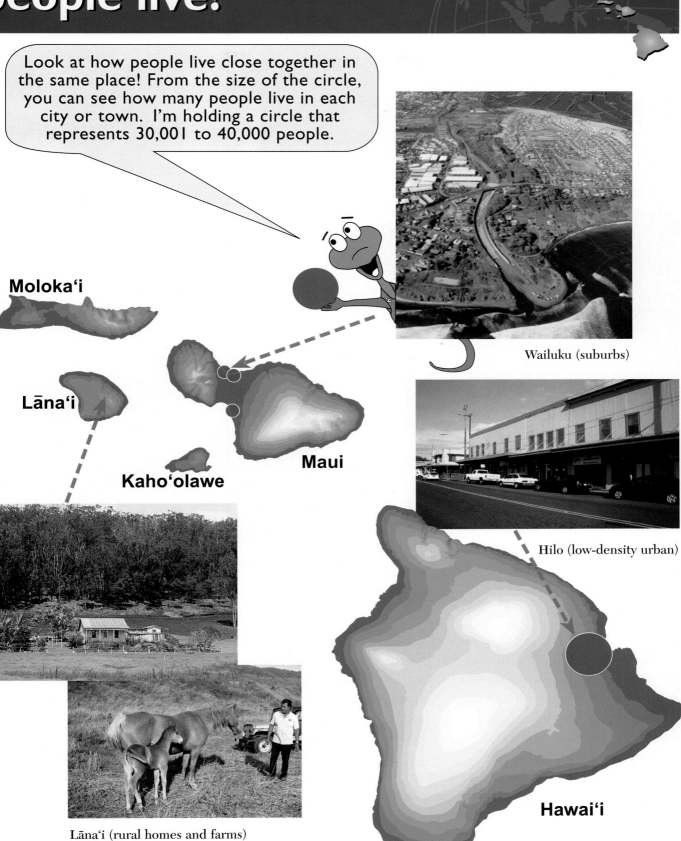

Moloka'i

Lāna'i

Kaho'olawe

Maui

Wailuku (suburbs)

Hilo (low-density urban)

Hawai'i

Lāna'i (rural homes and farms)

Kaua'i forest reserve

Hanauma Bay marine life conservation district

PROTECTED AREAS are places where human activity and development are limited in order to preserve special natural or cultural features for everyone's benefit. For example, forest reserves were created in steep mountain areas to ensure a continuous supply of pure drinking water and reduce soil erosion that might occur if the land was cleared. Wildlife sanctuaries, refuges, and natural areas reserves were established to protect native ecosystems and endangered species. Other places have been set aside as public parks so people can have areas for recreation (swimming, surfing, hiking, golf, and other outdoor activities).

Can you tell where the humpback whales live?

National marine sanctuary
(humpback whale)

20 miles
30 km

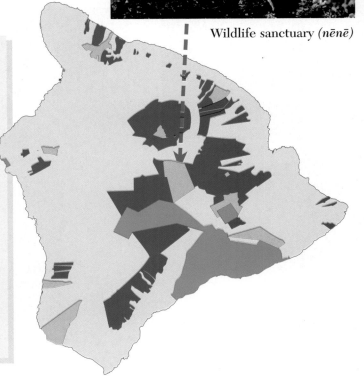

Wildlife sanctuary (*nēnē*)

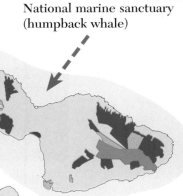

MAP KEY

national park

national wildlife refuge

national marine sanctuary (whale)

state forest reserve

state natural area reserve,
wildlife sanctuary, and marine
life conservation district and major
private preserves

major state and county park

Ni'ihau

Kaua'i

sugarcane

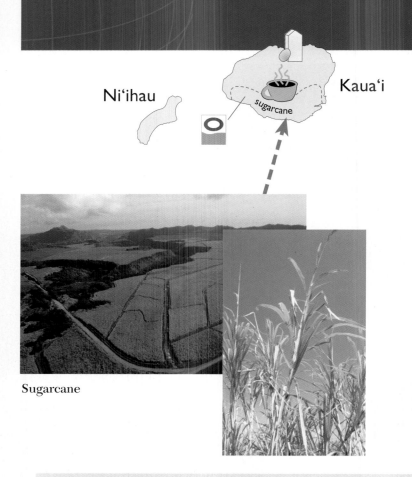

Sugarcane

O'ahu

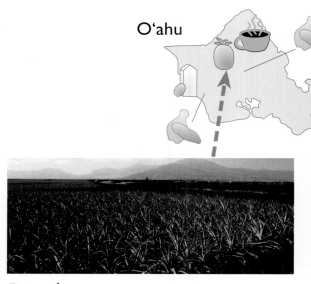

Pineapple

TRADITIONAL HAWAIIAN AGRICULTURE: The *Ahupua'a*

Forest

Breadfruit

>2000'

1000' to 2000'

sea level to 1000'

medicinal plants, bird feathers, vines, wood for building

banana, breadfruit

sugarcane, taro (kalo)

fishpond

the ahupua'a

Taro *(kalo)*

Long before sugar and pineapple were grown commercially, Hawaiians were SUBSISTENCE FARMERS. They grew crops and raised fish for their own use. Each *'ohana* farmed the land within their *ahupua'a*, which is the roughly pie-shaped setion of land that extended *mauka* (mountains) to *makai* (coast). The crops grown were suited to the different climate conditions along the slope. Typically, taro (*kalo*) was grown in lowland areas, and other crops, like sweet potato and breadfruit, were grown at higher elevations. In this way Hawaiians adapted their farming system to the conditions of the natural environment.

Many different crops can grow in our mild tropical climate. But land is expensive in Hawai'i, and we are far away from places that buy our products. The two main plantation crops for the past century, sugarcane and pineapple, have greatly declined in recent decades because of competition from lower-cost growers in other tropical areas of the world. Some specialized crops with high value, like macadamia nuts, coffee, papaya, and ginger, are still important agricultural EXPORTS from Hawai'i. Today we IMPORT most of our food from other parts of the world.

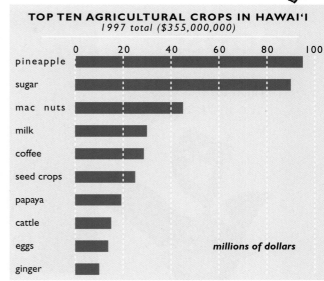

TOP TEN AGRICULTURAL CROPS IN HAWAI'I
1997 total ($355,000,000)

	0	20	40	60	80	100
pineapple						
sugar						
mac nuts						
milk						
coffee						
seed crops						
papaya						
cattle						
eggs						
ginger						

millions of dollars

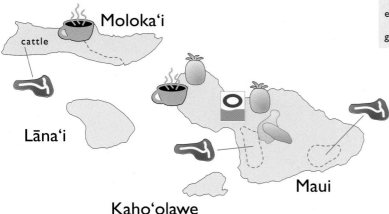

Moloka'i

cattle

Lāna'i

Kaho'olawe

Maui

Ginger farm

MAP KEY

pineapple

sugarcane

macadamia nuts

coffee

cattle

fruits & vegetables

dairy

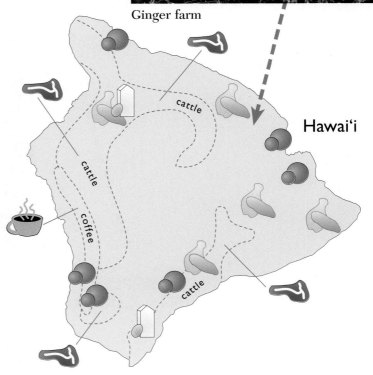

cattle

cattle

coffee

cattle

Hawai'i

FOODS!

My *muʻumuʻu* was made in Hawaiʻi!

Hui Hōʻike Honua

CALROSE RICE

SPAM

NORI- seaweed
(Japan)

CHOPSTICKS
(China)

SPAM®
(Minnesota)

RICE
(California)

Hawaiʻi

APPLE
(New Zealand)

OTHER THINGS!

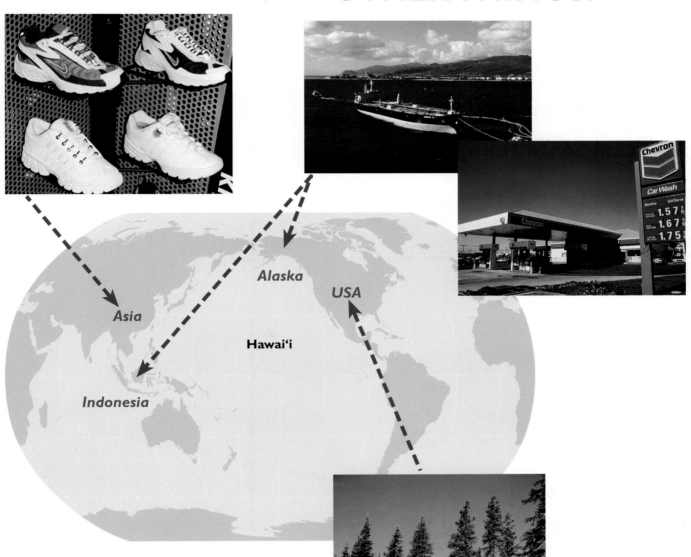

The ECONOMY of Hawai'i is based on import and export. We use money we get from the things we sell (exports) to buy things that are not made locally (imports). We buy petroleum (oil) from Indonesia and Alaska to run our electric plants and cars. Most of the foods we eat, clothes we wear, and things we use everyday are imported from somewhere else in the world. When people in one place buy from or sell to people in another place, we call this TRADE

41

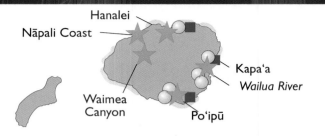

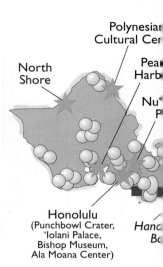

Polynesian
Cultural Center

North
Shore

Peal
Harb

Nu'
P

Honolulu
(Punchbowl Crater,
'Iolani Palace,
Bishop Museum,
Ala Moana Center)

Hanc
Be

Waimea Canyon

Waikīkī Beach

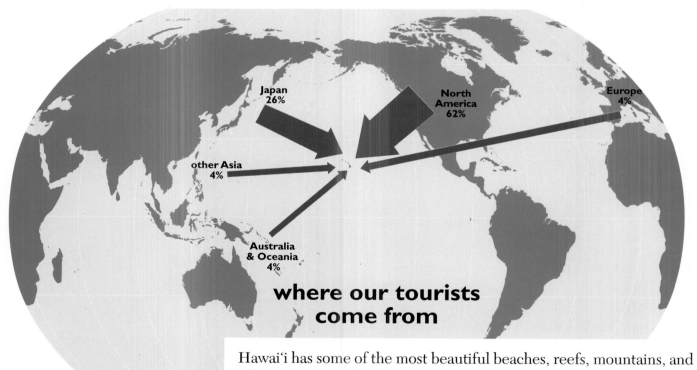

Japan
26%

North
America
62%

Europe
4%

other Asia
4%

Australia
& Oceania
4%

where our tourists come from

Hawaiʻi has some of the most beautiful beaches, reefs, mountains, and other scenery in the world. Just as important to visitors from around the world are Hawaiian music and dance and the *aloha* spirit of all the residents. The natural beauty and cultural diversity make Hawaiʻi a special place, for both tourists and residents.

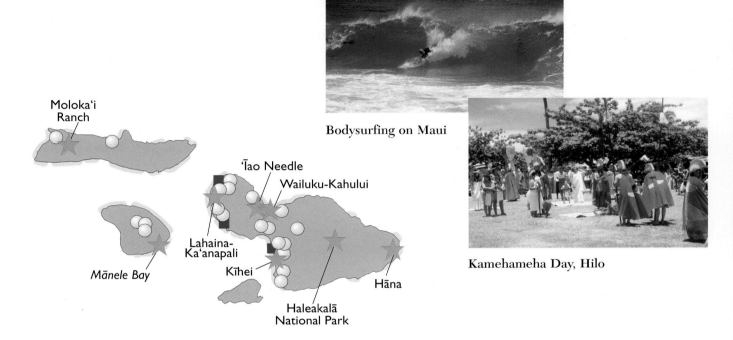

Bodysurfing on Maui

Kamehameha Day, Hilo

Moloka'i Ranch

'Īao Needle

Wailuku-Kahului

Lahaina-Ka'anapali

Mānele Bay

Kīhei

Haleakalā National Park

Hāna

Almost 7 million tourists come here each year and spend 10 billion dollars.

MAP KEY

⬭ major beaches

◼ major resort areas

★ tourist attractions

◯ major golf courses

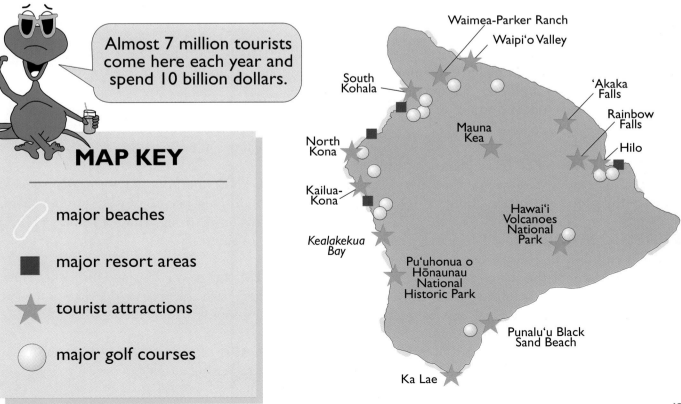

Waimea-Parker Ranch

Waipi'o Valley

South Kohala

'Akaka Falls

Rainbow Falls

Mauna Kea

North Kona

Hilo

Kailua-Kona

Hawai'i Volcanoes National Park

Kealakekua Bay

Pu'uhonua o Hōnaunau National Historic Park

Punalu'u Black Sand Beach

Ka Lae

Glossary

ALIEN SPECIES: a plant or animal that was brought to Hawai'i by people, either on purpose or by accident.

ATOLL: a string of low, sandy islands that enclose a shallow lagoon. Atolls are formed from coral reefs that grow in shallow tropical water where volcanic islands used to be before they were destroyed by erosion and sinking.

CARTOGRAPHER: a person who makes maps. Today most maps are made with the help of computers.

CONDENSATION: cooling of the air that changes water vapor (gas) to water droplets (liquid). Condensation is necessary to produce rainfall.

CONTINENT: one of the Earth's seven largest land areas: North America, South America, Europe, Asia, Africa, Australia, and Antarctica.

ECONOMY: the way a community is organized in order for people to work at different jobs and provide for their needs.

ECOSYSTEM: a group of plants and animals that live together (some eat others!) and depend on the physical resources (sunlight, water, and soil) of an area.

ENDANGERED SPECIES: plants or animals that are protected by federal and state law because they are threatened with extinction.

ENDEMIC SPECIES: a native plant or animal that is found only in Hawai'i and nowhere else in the world. Many of the native plants and animals that arrived in Hawai'i over the past several million years adapted to the special environments in Hawai'i and changed through evolution into new species. 'Alalā is an endemic species of crow, different from crows in other parts of the world.

EQUATOR: an imaginary line around the middle of the Earth halfway between the North and South poles. It is the 0 degree line for measuring latitude north or south.

EROSION: the wearing away of the land surface over time. Rocks and soil are carried away by gravity, flowing water, waves, glaciers, or wind.

ETHNIC GROUP: people who share a common cultural identity (language, customs, religion) and whose ancestors come from the same homeland.

EXPORTS: things we produce here and sell to people outside Hawai'i, like sugar, pineapple, macadamia nuts, and Hawaiian music.

GAZETTEER: a book or index containing geographical names and descriptions, arranged in alphabetical order.

GEOGRAPHER: a person who studies different places to learn about their natural environment and human society.

HACHURES: short lines on a map that show the location and direction of a steep slope.

HOT SPOT: a fixed point of high temperature in the Earth's mantle where rocks melt and erupt to form volcanoes at the surface.

HURRICANE: an intense storm that develops over warm tropical oceans during summer months. Hurricanes have strong winds 74 miles (119 km) per hour or more.

IMPORTS: things we buy and bring to Hawai'i from other parts of the world, like petroleum, apples, automobiles, and video games.

LANDSCAPE: all the features we see on the land, both natural and made by people.

LATITUDE: measurement (in degrees) of north-south location on the Earth's surface starting at the equator.

LEEWARD: the side of an island facing away from the trade winds, where rainfall is low.

LONG-DISTANCE DISPERSAL: the different natural ways that plants and animals could cross the Pacific Ocean to reach Hawai'i.

LONGITUDE: measurement (in degrees) of east-west location on the Earth's surface starting at the prime meridian.

MAGMA: rocks that have melted due to high temperature deep in the Earth's crust or mantle.

MAP KEY: a list that explains what the symbols and colors on a map mean.

MAP PROJECTION: a method of using lines on a flat map to represent the imaginary latitude and longitude lines on the globe.

MAP SCALE: the relationship between the distance on a map and the actual distance on the surface of the Earth.

MERIDIANS: north-south imaginary lines on the Earth's surface showing points of equal longitude.

MIGRATE: to move from one's place of birth and find a new home at a different place.

NATIVE SPECIES: a plant or animal that arrived and became established in Hawai'i by natural, long-distance dispersal without the help of people.

PACIFIC PLATE: a part of the Earth's crust under the Pacific Ocean that is made up of heavy, iron-rich rock. The Pacific Plate is moving slowly, carrying the Hawaiian Islands toward Asia.

PARALLELS: east-west imaginary lines on the Earth's surface showing points of equal latitude.

PRIME MERIDIAN: an imaginary line running from the North Pole to the South Pole that passes through Greenwich, near London, England. It is the 0 degree line for measuring longitude east and west.

SPATIAL DISTRIBUTION: the pattern showing where things are in an area.

SUBSISTENCE FARMER: a person who grows crops or raises animals mainly for use at home.

SUBURBS: an area around the center of a city where people live and play.

TERRAIN: the natural features of a piece of land, its shape and slope.

TRADE: buying things from or selling things to people in another place.

TRADE WINDS: strong winds in tropical latitudes that blow toward the equator. In Hawai'i the trade winds blow from the northeast.

TSUNAMI: a large ocean wave produced when energy is released during a submarine earthquake.

URBAN AREA: a place where many people live close together and work in shops, offices, factories, and hotels.

WINDWARD: the side of an island facing into the trade winds, where rainfall is high.

Gazetteer

For general Hawaiian place names and places of interest see the inside front cover.

For Pacific Basin and worldwide place names see page 18 and 48 and inside back cover.

Below is an alphabetical listing of other place names shown on maps in this atlas.

Abbreviations:
Ha=Hawai'i; K=Kaua'i; La=Lāna'i; Mo=Moloka'i; Ma=Maui; Oa=O'ahu; Inside front cover=IFC

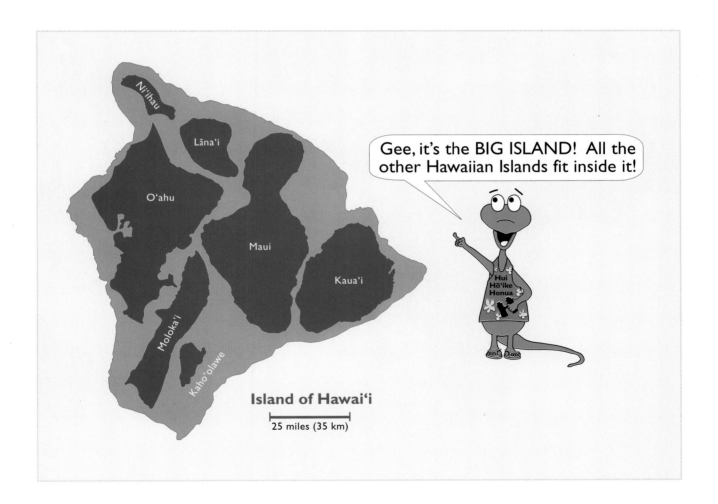

Gee, it's the BIG ISLAND! All the other Hawaiian Islands fit inside it!

Niʻihau
Lānaʻi
Oʻahu
Maui
Kauaʻi
Molokaʻi
Kahoʻolawe

Island of Hawaiʻi

25 miles (35 km)

World Map